MW01145575

For Wylder, my little Smitty Baby, who (to no surprise at all),
has kept me laughing since the day I met him.

This book is a product of a man who is continuously embarking on money-making endeavors at his family's expense, his wife who swears she's not resentful, and their almost five-month-old baby boy who hasn't learned enough words to protest.

Where Are You Going, Smitty Baby?
Text and Illustration Copyright 2009 by Meridith Smith

Published by must emote. & Smitty Baby
Clinton, OK
www.mustemote.com
www.smittybaby.com

Registered @ Library of Congress
ISBN-978-0-615-30279-9 / ISBN-10 0615302793 (hardcover)

Distributed by Smitty Baby
www.smittybaby.com

Photos shot at I Am Gravel Veins Studio by Caleb Wilkerson
www.iamgravelveins.com

Thanks to Corey Fuller, Jacob Sullivan, and Adam Smith for putting up with the questions.

Where are you going, Smitty Baby?

written and illustrated by
Meridith Smith

Happy reading!

Wyeder

and Meridith

Where are you going, Smitty Baby?

It looks like you have...

a floppy, yellow hat,
a pail with a shovel,
and glasses for the sun.

Let me see...

You're going to...

the beach!

Where are you going, Smitty Baby?

I can see that you have...

smart-looking glasses,
a tall stack of books,
and a card with your name on it.

I know...

The **library**, of course!

Where are you going, Smitty Baby?

You have...

nice, crisp money,

an empty tote bag,

and a long list of food.

I got it!

Where are you going, Smitty Baby?

I see that you are...

showing your muscles,
sporting your sneakers,
and giving your legs a good stretch!

Hmmm...

The gym!

I knew it!

Where are you going, Smitty Baby?

It looks like you have...

a fluffy, rainbow wig,
stripey socks,
and an elephant!

I know...

It's the **circus!**
And it looks like
a whole lot of fun!

Where are you going, Smitty Baby?

I see that you have...

a weird, shiny suit,
a map of outer space,
and a rocketship!

You're going to the **moon!**

WELCOME
to the
MOON

Where are you going, Smitty Baby?

You have...

a clear, plastic cap,

a squeaky little duck,

and a soft, **brown** towel.

That's right!

You're going to take a bath!

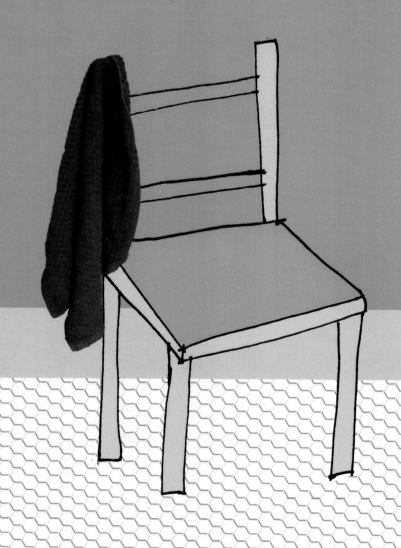

Where are you going, Smitty Baby?

It looks like you have...

a polka dot blanket,

a friendly monkey,

and a book.

I think...

You're going to bed!

the Night Night Book

Nighty night, Smitty Baby.

This book is a product of

SMITTY
BABY